Bashful
Ball Pythons

Kelly Doudna
AUTHOR

C.A. Nobens
ILLUSTRATOR

Consulting Editor, Diane Craig, M.A./Reading Specialist

A Division of ABDO

ABDO
Publishing Company

visit us at www.abdopublishing.com

Published by ABDO Publishing Company, a division of ABDO, P.O. Box 398166, Minneapolis, Minnesota 55439. Copyright © 2013 by Abdo Consulting Group, Inc. International copyrights reserved in all countries. No part of this book may be reproduced in any form without written permission from the publisher. SandCastle™ is a trademark and logo of ABDO Publishing Company.

Printed in the United States of America, North Mankato, Minnesota
102012
012013

 PRINTED ON RECYCLED PAPER

Editor: Liz Salzmann
Content Developer: Nancy Tuminelly
Cover and Interior Design and Production: Kelly Doudna, Mighty Media, Inc.
Photo Credits: Shutterstock, ThinkStock

Library of Congress Cataloging-in-Publication Data

Doudna, Kelly, 1963-
  Bashful ball pythons / by Kelly Doudna ; illustrator C.A. Nobens.
     p. cm. -- (Unusual pets)
  ISBN 978-1-61783-397-7
1. Ball pythons as pets--Juvenile literature. I. Nobens, C. A., ill. II. Title.
  SF459.S5D68 2013
  639.3'9678--dc23
                          2011050724

SandCastle™ Level: Transitional

SandCastle™ books are created by a team of professional educators, reading specialists, and content developers around five essential components—phonemic awareness, phonics, vocabulary, text comprehension, and fluency—to assist young readers as they develop reading skills and strategies and increase their general knowledge. All books are written, reviewed, and leveled for guided reading, early reading intervention, and Accelerated Reader® programs for use in shared, guided, and independent reading and writing activities to support a balanced approach to literacy instruction. The SandCastle™ series has four levels that correspond to early literacy development. The levels are provided to help teachers and parents select appropriate books for young readers.

| Emerging Readers (no flags) | Beginning Readers (1 flag) | Transitional Readers (2 flags) | Fluent Readers (3 flags) |

Contents

Unusual Pets

Unusual pets can be interesting and fun! Unusual pets might also eat unusual food. They might have special care needs. It is a good idea to learn about your new friend before bringing it home.

There are special laws for many unusual animals. Make sure the kind of pet you want is allowed in your city and state.

Ball Python Basics

Type of animal

Ball pythons are reptiles.

Adult size

3 to 5 feet (.9 to 1.5 m)

Life expectancy

20 to 30 years

Natural habitat

African **savannas** and
grasslands

Ball pythons are **docile** snakes. Justin's snake curls gently around his shoulders.

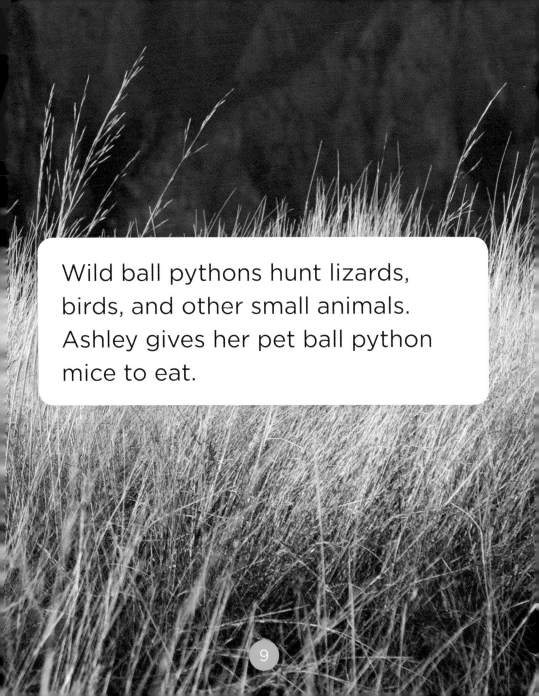

Wild ball pythons hunt lizards, birds, and other small animals. Ashley gives her pet ball python mice to eat.

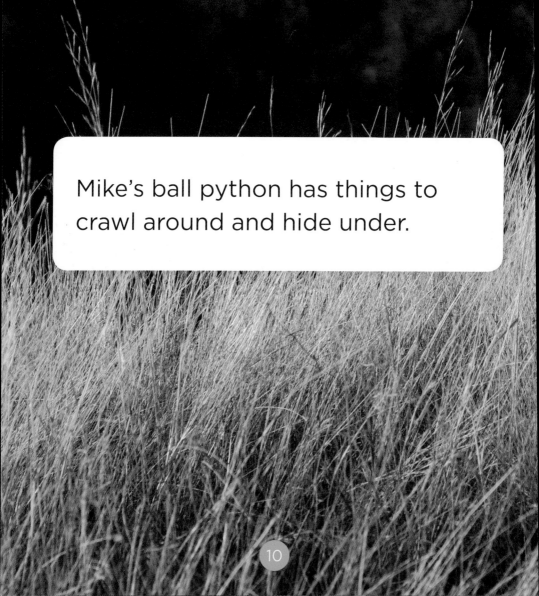

Mike's ball python has things to crawl around and hide under.

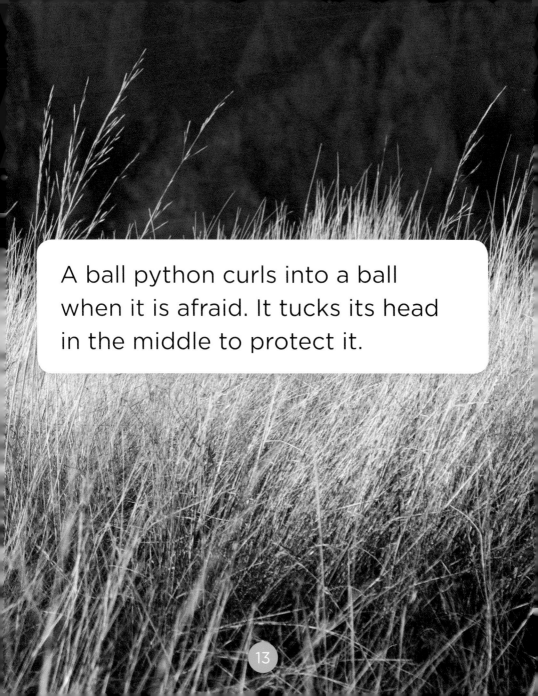

A ball python curls into a ball when it is afraid. It tucks its head in the middle to protect it.

A Ball Python Story

Stacy likes snakes
and has one as a pet.
Pete the ball python
is as gentle as they get.

When Pete and Stacy play,
Stacy makes a fist.
Pete crawls onto her arm
and coils around her wrist.

They go to the kitchen.
Stacy has a plan.
She pours a cup of pop
and gives Pete the can.

Pete coils around the can
and crushes till it's flat.
Stacy says, "Good snake!"
She gives his head a pat.

Now it's time for Stacy
to go get ready for bed.
She picks up the toothpaste.
An idea pops into her head.

She hands the tube to Pete
who gives it a small **squeeze**.
The toothpaste goes on her brush
as neatly as you please.

Stacy thinks that Pete
is an interesting friend.
They've had fun playing.
The day is at an end.

Stacy falls right to sleep.
She hugs her Teddy bear.
Pete curls up around her quilt.
The **fluff** flies everywhere!

Fun Facts

* Young ball pythons grow about one foot (30 cm) per year.

* In some African **cultures**, the ball python is thought of as a **symbol** of the earth.

* Ball pythons are also called royal pythons. This is because it's said that Cleopatra wore one around her wrist.

* Ball pythons are very good swimmers.

Ball Python Quiz

Read each sentence below. Then decide whether it is true or false!

1. Ball pythons are **docile** snakes.

2. A ball python curls into a ball to protect its head.

3. Pete crushes a plastic bottle in the kitchen.

4. Pete **squeezes** glue onto Stacy's toothbrush.

5. Stacy can't fall asleep.

Glossary

culture – the ideas, traditions, art, and behaviors of a group of people.

docile – calm and easy to control.

fluff – pieces of soft, light material, such as wool or cotton.

savanna – a grassland with few trees.

squeeze – to press or grip something tightly.

symbol – an object that stands for or represents something else.

tank – a large container for fish and reptiles to live in.